Monitoring

♥ Detect delays on your baby's first-year motor developments.

Bonding

♥ Spend quality time and bond with your baby while playing and exercising together.

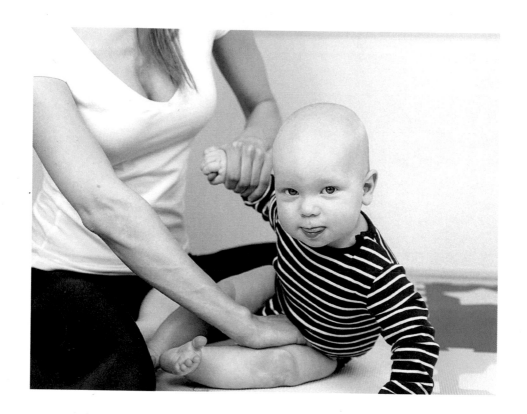

Exercise

💜 Learn tips and simple physiotherapy exercises on how to improve your baby's correct motor performance throughout the first-year milestones.

Development

♥ Easy exercises promote your baby's brain and motor development and help your baby to move easily through developmental milestones.

Security

♥ Increase developmental awareness and a sense of security.
Know when there is a need to turn to experts.

MONITORING
Detect delays on your baby's first-year motor developments.

BONDING
Spend quality time and bond with your baby while playing and exercising together.

EXERCISE
Learn tips and simple physiotherapy exercises on how to improve your baby's correct motor performance throughout the first-year milestones.

DEVELOPMENT
Easy exercises promote your baby's brain and motor development and help your baby to move easily through developmental milestones.

SECURITY
Increase developmental awareness and a sense of security. Know when there is a need to turn to experts.

Maarja Sade

My Active
Baby

Infant Physical Activities
for Motor Development,
Therapy, and Sensory Play

MY ACTIVE BABY
Infant Physical Activities for Motor Development,
Therapy, and Sensory Play
By Maarja Sade

Translated and edited by Wiedemanni Translation Company

The Estonian Association of Physiotherapists has approved
all of the exercises shown in this book.

Cover design **Jaak Rüütel** and **Ellen Leene**
Interior design **Ellen Leene**
Photos **Kätlin Kask**

Copyright © Maarja Sade and Helios Kirjastus Ltd, 2020

ISBN 978-9949-610-71-6

Publishing house Helios Kirjastus

Maarja Sade

My Active
Baby

Infant Physical Activities
for Motor Development,
Therapy, and Sensory Play

Foreword

☆ The birth of my son was one of the most amazing, empowering experiences of my life. I had been looking forward to meeting him, dreaming about him, carrying him for nine months. During my pregnancy, I did my best to make him feel secure in his temporary home. I followed the doctor's advice, such as daily balanced meals and exercise – I took prenatal yoga classes and other exercise classes for expectant mothers. I attended information lectures for expectant families, did a lot of research before buying a pram, a carry cot and other items that babies need – I did everything to be adequately equipped for what lay ahead. I packed my hospital bag a month before the baby was due.

And finally, my son arrived. On a day when I least expected it, because the date – 8/8 – seemed like a cliché. I did not believe for a moment that he would choose that day. But then, a week before the due date, our little miracle was born.

With hindsight, no matter how well prepared I was for the arrival of my baby, when he was born I felt that I had been thrown into unknown waters. It was an extraordinary and new experience even for me, someone who is working with babies on a daily basis. Not for nothing is it said that you are not born a parent; you become one over time. I was surprised at just how much attention a newborn needs.

I had a zillion questions. When and how much should he sleep? How should I feed my baby to ease colic? How and how often should I clean the baby's umbilical stump? Can I pick him up and cuddle him or feed him on every whimper? How do I dress my baby to make sure that he is neither too hot nor too cold? I had so many questions in my mind.

The only area I felt confident enough was related to my job – infant physiotherapy. When I think back to that time, I believe that my job really came in handy to me as a first time mother. At the same time I have to admit that my son was a great teacher and I am grateful that he chose me as his mother. I feel that he made me a much better physiotherapist than I used to be.

It is an invaluable experience, observing my child develop and grow during his first year of life. You cannot compare children because their family backgrounds and personalities, as well as speeds of development are different. Nonetheless, I can now put myself in the shoes of worrying parents and relate to them.

I hope that this book will help you whenever you have questions about your baby's development. Exercising regularly with your baby will facilitate the development of the baby's brain and spatial skills. Doing things together paves the way for parent-baby bonding and enables you to become a confident parent.

This book divides the skills and exercises between four age groups – from birth to 3 months, from 3 to 6 months, from 6 to 9 months and from 9 months to the first independent steps. Remem-

ber that each baby develops at their own pace. The age groups are indicative. In real life, learning a skill may take about a month less or more compared to the average.

For example, babies learn to roll over from back to stomach at three to six months and on average at four or five months. This means that subsequent skills may also be learned earlier or later than the average. If your child masters rolling from back to stomach at three months, he or she may start crawling earlier than those children who learn the movement from back to stomach at five months.

Infant development over the first 12 months of life is very rapid. A helpless bundle will transform into a walking toddler. Children are programmed to go through all stages of development. No important stage of motor development should be skipped in order to speed up walking. Each child will start walking when he or she is ready. Here, you will find activities and recommendations for supporting your baby through all of the important milestones of motor development. Through everyday caring for your baby, you will build the bond with your baby and become a more confident parent. And your baby will learn that he or she can always rely on you.

Contents

0-3 months

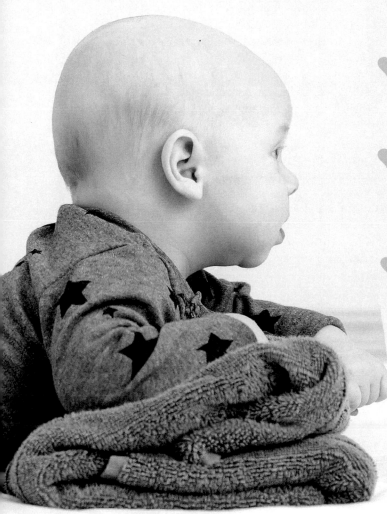

Important motor skill milestones:

♥ **2 months on average – postural symmetry:** the baby is able to hold their head in midline for longer, makes eye contact, smiles responsively, coos and babbles.

♥ **2.5 months on average – bringing hands to midline:** the baby reaches for a toy and/or the face of a familiar person.

♥ **2.5 months on average – head control:** the baby will have developed sturdier neck muscles and their head needs less support.

♥ **3 months on average – propping up on forearms in the prone position:** the baby is able to bear their body weight in the prone position, raises head and looks around.

Postural symmetry

The typical spine posture of a newborn is asymmetrical. Asymmetrical head and body position shows head predilection (i.e., newborn's preferred head rotation toward one side). The baby is yet unable to bring their head to midline and make eye contact, i.e. to maintain a symmetric posture. Primitive newborn reflexes (the asymmetrical tonic neck reflex (ATNR)) and weak neck muscles prevent the baby from bringing their head to midline. When the face is turned to one side, the arm and leg on the side to which the face is turned extend and the arm and leg on the opposite side flex. The positions of arms and legs can cause the spine to curve. This is often called the fencing position. While this reflex lasts until the baby is about 4 months, its impact already starts to weaken at about 1-2 months of age as the child's neck muscles strengthen. As the neck muscles strengthen, the head and neck will resist the tonic- neck-reflex inclination and the child can hold their head in midline. In the first couple of months of a baby's life, weak neck muscles may cause head predilection. Therefore, it is important to check the position of the baby's head.

Weak neck muscles and ATNR prevent the baby from turning their head from left to right and vice versa. While the baby will follow your movements and turn their head towards the source of light or sound, it is a very strenuous exercise.

In the first month of life, babies are stimulated by bright light and different sounds. It is important to be aware of the location of the external stimuli the infant is exposed to (TV, windows, lights, vivid wallpaper/walls, toys and yourself). If all of these stimuli are on the baby's right, the baby may prefer turning their head to that side because there is nothing interesting on the other side. You should also make sure that the baby is stimulated from both sides, by regularly switching your baby's position in their bed and approaching and picking up the baby from both sides. Holding-side preference means that the infant is looking to the right the majority of time. If the preference is very strong, your baby may even protest when you put him or her down on the other side or turn their head. If the child mainly looks to one side, it may cause asymmetric skull, cheekbone and jawbone deformities. This is because the infant's bones are very soft and pliable.

This head deformation is not the only problem caused by holding-side preference. The child may also develop body asymmetry, meaning that the baby prefers one side of their body (favours one hand when grabbing objects, only rolls over one side, and so forth). The muscles on one side of the body become stronger than on the opposite side. Imbalance of muscles in the back may result in scoliosis, in which the spine develops unusual curves. It is very important in the first month to check your baby's positions and environment in order to facilitate symmetric development.

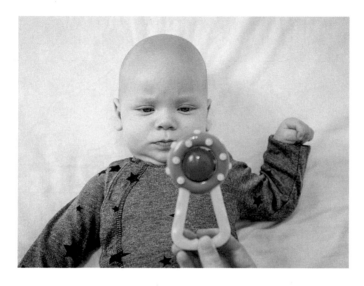

Be careful about your baby handling practices. Change sides while holding and carrying your baby and use both hands when picking the baby up for washing their bottom. I have to admit that I broke that rule repeatedly by force of habit. It was much more convenient to lift my son to my left shoulder to burp him and to turn him on his left side to wipe his bottom. This caused a minor gaze preference but nothing that a mum/physical therapist cannot handle. I just had to constantly remind myself to use the other arm and body side and the gaze preference disappeared in a week.

Helping the baby to develop a symmetric posture is something many parents do instinctively. Every parent wants their baby to look at them, smile and communicate. Therefore, it is not hard to achieve that the baby holds their head in midline. It comes naturally to us – using the positions that enable us to communicate with our baby face-to-face. Trust your inner wisdom and communicate with your baby, while holding their attention in the midline.

Tips for parents:

♥ In the first months, put your baby to bed alternatively on each side (one nap on the right side, another on the left side). This enables you to control the pressure of the surface on your baby's skull and face and to prevent deformities and side preference.

♥ Be mindful of the environment in which your baby spends most of their time. Make sure that any objects that may interest the baby are not only on one side. If your baby consistently lies in the same place, reverse the position of their head and legs so that the stimuli from the environment around the baby come from a different side.

♥ Remember, a toy is your baby's most important "tool". Start introducing toys early on by placing them above the baby's chest, in the midline and within reach. Use a baby activity mat.

♥ Use different techniques to hold your baby. In the first months of their life, your baby needs closeness and contact. When holding your baby, alternate between the left and right arm, place the baby on the stomach on your arms, carry them on your shoulder or with the baby facing away from you (see 'Holding the baby' on page 114-119). When you pick up your baby (for example, to wash the baby's bottom), turn him or her both to the right and to the left.

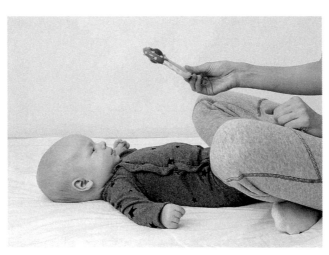

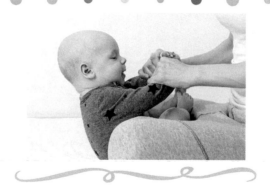

Head control

When your baby is born, their neck muscles are very weak and you need to support his or her head every time you pick your baby up. Avoid sudden back and forth movements of the baby's head because it may damage their spine and spinal cord. In the first months, your baby will rely on you to support their head and neck when you pick your baby up or hold them. As the baby develops sturdier neck muscles, their head needs less external support.

Starting from the second month, support your baby's head as much as necessary and as little as possible. This will help the baby to strengthen their neck muscles and to develop head control. For a baby to achieve head control, both the neck flexor and extensor muscles must strengthen. Many parents are familiar with the exercises performed during monthly visits to their GP to test their baby's neck muscles. Neck tone is assessed by doing the neck traction test. Here hands are firmly grasped and the infant is pulled into the semi-reclined position. For most parents, this is the first thing they remember from their visit to their GP and they eagerly start to strengthen their baby's neck flexor muscles. However, the other muscles – extensor muscles – are often ignored. For your baby to develop firm head control and strong extensor muscles, give your baby plenty of tummy time, i.e. your baby on their stomach. Not spending enough time lying on the tummy may cause a delay in the development of all subsequent motor skills.

Tips for parents:

♥ Starting from the second month, support your baby's head as much as necessary and as little as possible.

♥ When picking up your baby, do it from the side. This will strengthen the baby's flexor muscles. Remember to pick your baby up from both sides alternatively!

♥ Do exercises to strengthen the baby's neck flexor and extensor muscles.

Bringing hands
to midline

After your baby has learned to keep their head in midline and look you in the eyes for an extended period, they will start practicing an important new skill. It is time to start with the baby's most important job – play. At first, the game is very simple. The baby tries to lift their arms up towards the hanging toy. In the first months, the motions are spontaneous and uncoordinated. The baby is not able to control their arms. Gradually, your baby will learn, through trial and error, to bring their hands to midline. Perhaps you see your baby aimlessly moving their arms and legs – they are practicing to learn a new skill. Flailing arms accidentally touch a toy hanging overhead. The toy swings and maybe even makes a sound. This attracts the baby's attention. How can I make it happen again? The baby flails their arms in an attempt to make the toy swing or make a sound. Amazing! I did it again! Aimless movement of arms strengthens muscles.

At about 2.5 months, the infant's arm muscles are strong enough and the shoulder joint stable enough for the child to bring their arms intentionally into midline. Putting your child on their tummy also has an important role in the stabilisation of the shoulder joints. In order to learn to bring his or her arms into midline, the child should be interested in and have an opportunity to pat a toy, attempting to make it move or emit a sound. You can help by making sure that the toy is in the child's midline within their reach.

There are multiple tools to make it easier. I would recommend a play mat and a bouncy seat with an activity arch. If in doubt, prefer the play mat to the bouncy seat. Do not leave your infant in the bouncy seat for extended amounts of time. Being in a bouncy seat means that babies are spending less time developing floor mobility and are less eager to learn new skills. Let's face it – it is so easy to lie there with all interesting objects within reach and mummy and daddy in the field of vision. If your child is born with a calm and relaxed personality, they may lose any interest in learning to roll or play on their stomach.

While lying on their back on the play mat, the baby can practise bringing two hands together at the midline of the body. The toys dangle down from your baby's play mat arches in the midline of the body within the baby's reach and the baby can move freely and learn new skills. Remember that boredom plays a big role in learning new skills. When the baby is lying in a bouncy seat, mummy and daddy and the whole room are in the baby's field of vision. When the baby is lying on their back on a play mat, all they can see is the ceiling and the dangling toys. The baby gets bored and starts looking for ways to change position, which means that the child starts exercising their muscles in order to roll over.

Tips for parents:

- ♥ Hold an interesting toy in the midline of your baby's body. Make sure that the toy is within the baby's reach.

- ♥ Move your baby's hands – play clapping and patting games, such as "pat-a-cake", or try boxing movements.

- ♥ For the baby to bring their hands voluntarily into midline, objects of interest should be dangling within the baby's reach in the midline of the body. Toys can be attached to the car seat or pram. Use a play mat with activity arch to encourage your baby to bring their hands together.

Propping up on forearms in the prone position

At about three months, your baby will learn to prop him or herself up on their elbows and forearms for a short period of time. Learning this skill requires help because the baby is yet not able to roll independently from back to stomach.

Tummy time is the time the baby spends on their stomach, playing and discovering the surrounding environment (not the time the baby sleeps in the prone position; in the first couple of months the baby should sleep alternatively on each side). As a physical therapist of infants, I often see parents who are afraid or reluctant to put their baby on their stomach to play, which may cause problems with learning important motor skills (such as rolling, belly crawl, cross crawl, etc.). The main reasons why parents are reluctant to put their baby on his or her stomach are that their baby protests against being in the prone position or that the parents do not know how to do it in a right way.

You can start putting your baby on their tummy right after birth. Cradle your baby on their tummy on your chest because it is softer and easier on the baby's umbilical cord stump. After the stump dries up and falls off, you can start putting your baby on their stomach on the changing table, bed, exercise ball or play mat.

It is important to start tummy time as early as possible. In the beginning, put your baby on their tummy for 20 seconds at a time, several times a day (at least three to five times). Gradually increase the length of time your baby spends on their stomach. Being on the stomach strengthens the extensor muscles of neck and body. Stronger neck muscles facilitate head control. Strong body muscles are essential in rolling, belly crawling, cross crawling, maintaining balance while seated, etc. Supporting on forearms strengthens the child's shoulder muscles, helping to develop the skills of bringing hands together and grasping.

Babies who dislike playing on their stomach or don't get enough tummy time may fall behind in achieving developmentally appropriate motor skills milestones (such as rolling, belly crawling, cross crawling, sitting up, sitting with good balance, etc.). Tummy time develops the groups of muscles necessary for these activities. In addition to delayed motor development, babies who do not spend enough time on their stomach may develop flat head syndrome, which makes the back or side of baby's head appear flattened. The back or side of a baby's head flattens because the baby spends extended periods of time on their back with the head against a flat surface. This is because the infant's bones are very soft and malleable.

Parents are often reluctant to place their baby on his or her stomach because the baby dislikes it and protests. Nobody wants their baby to cry! It should be remembered that anything new is initially unfamiliar and difficult for your baby. Spending time on their stomach is essential for

the development of motor skills. Newborns have very weak neck and back muscles. Lifting their head and stretching the back in the prone position takes huge effort. When the baby spends time on their stomach, his or her back, neck and shoulder girdle muscles strengthen gradually and the baby does not object being on their tummy and is able to play for an extended period in this position.

Remember! Practice makes perfect. When your baby is awake, put them on their belly as often as possible. Do not be discouraged by the initial protests and give up putting your baby in the prone position. After all, exercising is supposed to be slightly strenuous. Being on the belly for a short time, yet often, is better than nothing.

I, too, had to face the biggest nightmare for any physical therapist. In the first months of his life, my son suffered from gas pains and a vast amount of my time and effort were spent trying to ease his discomfort. I noticed that he did not enjoy being on his tummy. He refused to be on his stomach even for a very short period of time. Since gas pains caused my baby so much discomfort and grumpy mood, I was reluctant to make his life even more difficult.

When the pain dissipated, I resumed putting him on his stomach for some 20 seconds at a time. I did it dozens of times each day. I gradually extended the tummy time and used various activities to help my son to learn to enjoy being on his stomach. His favourite exercises were balancing on my lap and activities on the exercise ball. Systematic exercises and putting my son on his tummy whenever he was awake paid off – after a month he agreed to be in the prone position for five minutes in a row. It all went uphill from there. No problems with learning to pivot, crawl on his belly or on his hands and knees.

Tips for parents:

♥ You can start putting your baby on their tummy right after birth. The sooner you start the more readily your baby accepts being on their tummy as a natural position.

♥ Do not expect your baby to be able to be on their tummy for several minutes from the start. Put your baby on their tummy often and for short periods of time to avoid creating unpleasant associations for the baby. Remember to take a break when your baby becomes distressed. Put your baby on their back and try again after a couple of minutes.

♥ There are ways to help your baby be on their tummy. The easiest way is to use a rolled up towel or a nursing pillow. Place a rolled towel (or a pillow) under your baby's chest so that their torso is higher than his or her bottom. When the baby's pelvis is supported, it is easier for them to lift their head and train the extensor muscles of the neck and back. A good idea is to use an exercise ball (with the diameter of about 65 cm).

♥ To practise being on the stomach, place your baby on your chest with their head facing yours as often as possible. While you are in the semi-reclined position and your baby is placed on you, chest to chest, their head is higher than their bottom. The gravity centre of the baby's body moves down and it is easier for the baby to lift their head. Holding your baby chest to chest is another opportunity to train the baby's muscles. Put your baby on your shoulder (in the so-called 'burping position') to train their body and torso muscles.

♥ Put your baby on a hard surface on their stomach, lay down with your head facing theirs and play with them. Babies learn by imitating. Being on your stomach and distracting your baby from the labour of the exercise is an excellent way to extend their tummy time.

♥ If your baby dislikes being on their tummy, try to distract them. Use a toy or a rattle to help your baby enjoy their tummy time; give your baby a mirror to look at, play music, clap your hands or talk to them.

"I knew when I met you an adventure was going to happen."

Exercises
0-3 months

- 💜 Practise bringing head to midline
- 💜 Practise bringing hands to midline
- 💜 Strengthen neck muscles
- 💜 Practise propping up on forearms in the prone position

Practise bringing head to midline:

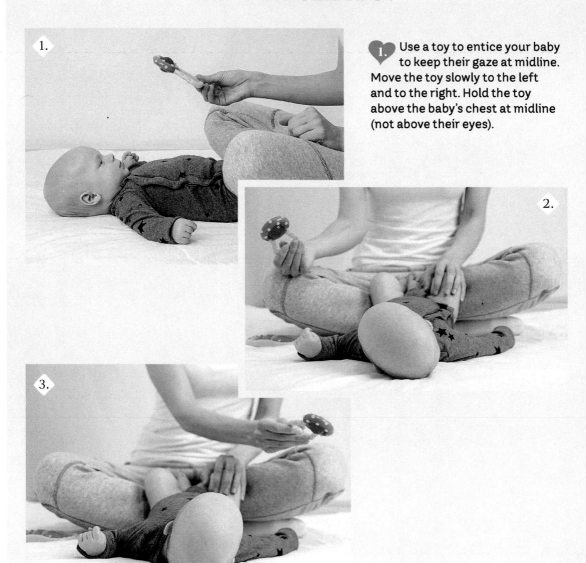

1. Use a toy to entice your baby to keep their gaze at midline. Move the toy slowly to the left and to the right. Hold the toy above the baby's chest at midline (not above their eyes).

1.

2. Cushion your baby's head with your hands and bend his or her head slightly forward. Talk to your baby and try to make them fix their gaze at you.

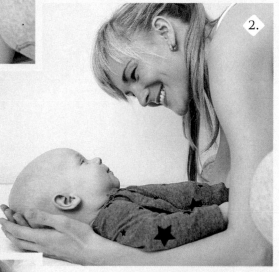

2.

3.

Tip!

To train tracing, move your head to the right and to the left.

1.

2.

3. Put your baby on your lap. Show your baby toys or talk or sing to them. To train tracing, move your head to the right and to the left.

Practise bringing hands to midline:

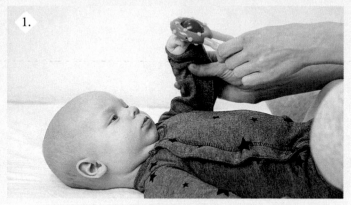

1.

❤ **1.** Place a toy in the midline of the baby's body, within their reach. In turns, bring your baby's left and right hand to the toy. Let the baby try to touch the toy independently.

2.

3.

Strengthen neck muscles:

1.

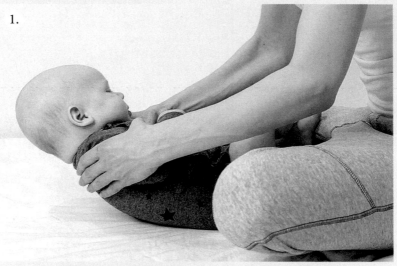

2.

1. Hold your baby with your thumbs on the baby's chest and your fingers on the baby's shoulder blades. Bring the baby into a semi-sitting position and slowly lower your baby on their back. When lowering the baby, you can support the back of their head with your fingers to prevent the head from falling back.

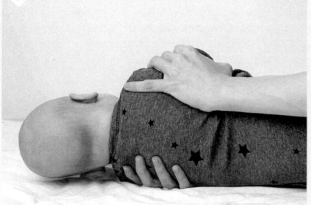

1.

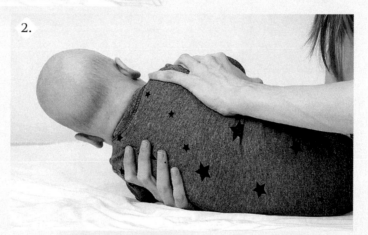

2. The baby is on their back. Put your right hand under the baby's left armpit. Put your left hand on the baby's right shoulder. Turn the baby to their left side and lift their head. Maintain this position and repeat with the other side.

2.

3.

Tip!

Always pick your child up the same way to strengthen their neck muscles through everyday activities. Note! Remember to use both sides of the body when picking your baby up.

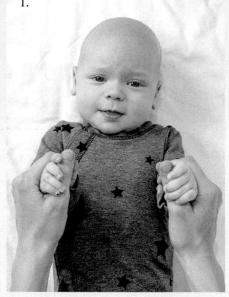

1.

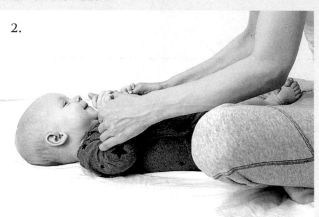

3. Put your thumbs in your baby's palms and grab their forearms. Slowly bring the baby into a semi-sitting position and then lower them on their back.

2.

3.

4. Place your baby with his or her back to your chest. Lean your baby forward and maintain this position, then draw him or her back against you. Repeat the exercise with the baby's sides.

Practise propping up on forearms in the prone position:

1. Put your baby on your lap so that their legs reach the floor. Make sure the baby is supporting on their forearms. Hold up a toy to make the baby to look up and stretch their neck and back.

2.

1.

2.

2. Place a rolled up towel under the baby's chest. Make sure your baby is propping up on their forearms. Hold up a toy to make the baby to look up and stretch their neck and back.

Tip!

You can use a stiff pillow or a nursing pillow instead of a rolled up towel.

3.

3. Put your baby on an exercise ball. Hold his or her arms so that the baby is propped up on their forearms. Move the ball slowly to the left and to the right.

1.

2.

3.

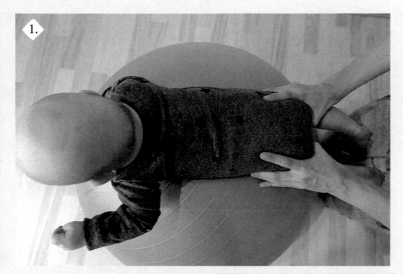

4. Put your baby on an exercise ball. Hold your baby's thighs so that your fingers are on their buttocks. Move the ball slowly forward. Let the baby stretch his or her neck and back and move the ball slowly back.

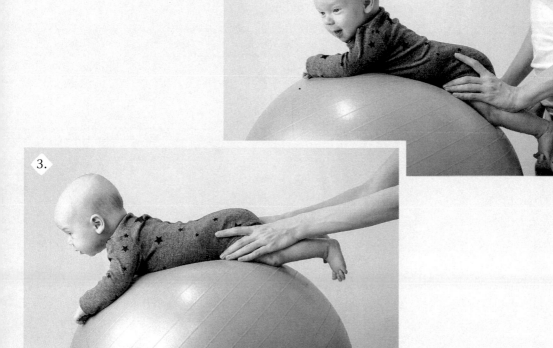

3-6 months

Important motor skill milestones:

- **4 months on average – grasping objects:**
  your baby can voluntarily grasp an object.
  Make sure that the baby is using both hands.

- **4-5 months on average – rolling from back to stomach:**
  your baby can independently roll from back to stomach,
  but not from stomach to back. Make sure that the baby
  rolls over on each side.

- **5 months on average – propping up on wrists in in the prone
  position:** your baby props on wrists, instead of forearms. His or
  her body is more stretched out. Fingers may still be bent into
  the palm (hands are clenched in a fist).

- **5 months on average – pivoting on stomach:**
  your baby starts to slowly pivot around on their stomach.
  Make sure the baby pivots both to the right and to the left.

- **6-7 months on average – crawling:**
  your baby is able to move forward on their stomach. Crawling is
  defined as any type of moving in which the tummy is on the floor.
  Sometimes babies crawl backwards before crawling forwards.

Voluntary grasping

By around 4 months, your baby will be able to grasp a toy voluntarily. While babies can grasp right after they are born, this is an involuntary reflex, rather than – as many parents assume – an intentional movement. Palmar grasp reflex is a primitive reflex..

When you place your finger in your infant's hand, their fingers will close reflexively, as your finger is grasped via palmar grasp. This involuntary movement should gradually disappear and is replaced by voluntary grasp by the time a child turns about 4 months old. Voluntary grasping means that the child decides when to open and close their hands to grasp an object. For instance, when the baby sees an interesting toy, they reach their hands and grasp the toy, bring it closer to their face or put it into their mouth to learn more about it.

To grasp, the baby's shoulder joints must be stable. If the baby is not able to reach towards an object, such as a toy dangling in front of them, they cannot grasp it. Therefore, it is important to place your child in a prone position to strengthen their shoulder muscles so that the baby is able to bring their arms and hands up against gravity and grasp a toy. Before learning to grasp, your baby should be able to bring their arms and hands up against gravity into midline. After learning to grasp, infants initially tend to use the ulnar side of their hand (pinky and ring fingers) more. Gradually, more fingers are involved, while the thumb is extended and does not assist with grasp.

At about 10 months, babies start to actively use their index finger (pointing at objects, pressing on buttons with their index finger, poking various cavities. Eventually, the thumb is also involved in grasping. The baby starts using the pincer grasp – using the index finger and thumb in concert to pick up small objects. Simultaneously with the pincer grab, your child will start to use the three finger grasp (thumb, index finger, and middle finger). When the baby has learned the pincer grab and the three finger grasp, parents must be particularly attentive about the small objects their child may pick up. If the baby has toddler siblings that play with toys containing small parts, parents must bear in mind that the baby can grab these small parts and put them into their mouth. These parts are a choking hazard to your child.

Tips for parents:

- ♥ Stroke the palms of your baby's hands to open fingers.

- ♥ If your baby likes playing with water, hold their hand and pat water. Water helps to relax muscles and stretch fingers.

- ♥ If your baby's hands are still clenched in fists most of the time at about 4 months, consult your GP. The baby may experience muscle tensions that prevent them from reaching the developmental milestones.

- ♥ Place interesting toys within your baby's reach.

Rolling from back to stomach

After your baby has acquired the above motor skills, they will want to move more. Lying on their back and watching, touching and grabbing toys is no longer enough. The child will start to roll from back to side and eventually manages to roll over on their stomach.

I would like to remind parents that while your baby is tiny in their first months of life and seems immobile, you will never know when exactly they decide to roll over or shift their body. Remember that the floor – playing on a play mat, blanket or carpet – is always the safest place for activities. If you leave your child unattended on a sofa, bed or changing table, they may - sooner or later - roll over, fall and get seriously hurt. Do not leave your baby on an elevated surface unattended – not even for a second! Remember that children can move spontaneously and change their position from the day they are born.

Before your baby learns to roll from back to stomach they will start doing bizarre movements on their back. He or she will try to lift their legs up. By bringing their legs up against gravity your baby gets to know their body and trains the flexor muscles of their body. By around 4 months, your baby will be able to touch their knees with their hands. At 5 months your baby will discover and start grabbing their toes. Some even try to fit their toes into their mouth. They do this to strengthen the flexor muscles of their torso and to prepare for rolling over.

Another weird movement that emerges at about 3 to 4 months is pulling forward and lifting their head. For instance, when you hold them on your lap in a semi-reclined position.

At 5 months, your baby is able to lift their head when lying on a smooth surface. Sometimes parents tend to misinterpret that movement. You may think that your baby is trying to sit up but in reality he or she is doing this to strengthen the flexor muscles of their torso and to prepare for rolling over. After your child has discovered stretching, avoid leaving them in the bouncy seat for extended periods of time. If your infant is strapped into the rocker they cannot learn the movements required for rolling over. He or she cannot turn on their side and continue rolling on their stomach. Naturally, it is easier for the baby to exercise the stomach muscles while lying in the bouncy seat because it is easier to pull forward from a semi-reclined position. However, if the baby pulls forward for an extended period of time the stomach muscles may become tense and painful. Just like your muscles after strenuous exercising. As a physical therapist I recommend to only use the bouncy seat when it is strictly necessary. Put your child on a play mat or blanket to play whenever possible.

Another important aspect in learning to roll over is to ensure that your child rolls over both sides. If the baby prefers to roll over one side only, place an interesting object on the opposite side and help the baby to roll over that side.

Tips for parents:

- Show your baby their toes and knees to encourage them to start lifting their legs against gravity.

- Pick the baby up from his or her side. This will teach rolling movements through everyday activities. Remember to use both sides of the body when picking your baby up.

- Place toys on your baby's sides to encourage them to roll from back to side.

- Limit the use of aiding tools and let your child play on a play mat, blanket or carpet so that the child can move freely and learn to roll over.

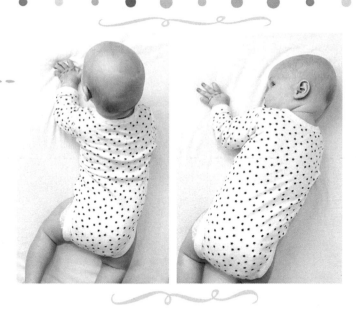

This is what happened to my son – because it was more convenient to hold him on my right arm when washing his bottom he developed a gaze preference to the left. So I turned him on his left side during changing. We got rid of the gaze preference rather quickly and he learned to bring both hands to midline to grasp a toy but his body was still used to turning to the left.

At first he rolled only over his left side. I started to encourage him to roll from back to stomach over his right side. It did not take long for him to learn to roll over both sides.

If your baby has learned to roll over but he or she does it over one side only, try to encourage them to roll over on both sides. Otherwise one side of their body will become stronger, which may cause muscle imbalance and lead to scoliotic changes in the spinal posture.

Propping up on wrists in the prone position

At about 5 months your baby will start raising their chest higher and higher while on their stomach. Propping up on elbows is not enough – your baby wants to see higher and farther and starts to push up on their wrists. Propping up on wrists means that the child's elbows are in front of their shoulders, the child stretches their arms and supports on their wrists. His or her hands may still be clenched in fists.

To encourage your baby to prop up on their wrists, put them on their stomach and place toys higher up in front of them. The baby will start pulling up their torso. While learning to prop up on wrists and pivoting, your baby may spontaneously "fall" from stomach to back. This is because he or she stretches one hand and their body weight falls on one side, making your baby roll from stomach to back. While such movement is initially often involuntary, it can quickly develop into intentional rolling from stomach to back. However, there are two important aspects that parents should take into account. First, to soften the fall, place your baby on a play mat or blanket, not on a hard floor surface. Doing so prevents an unpleasant experience for your baby. Second, if you notice that your baby 'falls' on one side only, that side of their body may be stronger than the other side. Massage your baby to reduce muscle tension and use exercises to strengthen the muscles of the weaker side of their body. The best exercise is shifting body weight to the weaker side of the body while the baby is on his or her stomach or shifting body weight alternatively from one side to the other while the baby is on the exercise ball.

Tips for parents:

♥ If your baby is yet not able to roll from back to stomach, place them on their tummy as often as possible so that they can learn how to prop up on their wrists.

♥ Put your baby on their stomach and hold a toy slightly above their field of vision to encourage the baby to stretch their torso.

♥ Make sure that your baby supports equally on both sides of their body (on both wrists) and does not 'fall' spontaneously on one side only.

Pivoting on stomach

Pivoting on the stomach is a skill that is often overlooked by parents. This skill is essential for the child to learn shifting their body weight from one side to the other and thus to learn to roll over. If the baby does not know how to shift their body weight, they will not learn to crawl. After the baby has learned to roll over, parents are often eager to teach the baby to move forward on their stomach. Pivoting means, however, moving the body in a circle around its axis – just like a spinner.

Without learning to pivot the baby cannot learn to move forward because moving forward requires shifting body weight from one side to the other. Pivoting helps to develop the movement of the baby's pelvis. By pivoting, the baby learns to lean their pelvis forward and backward.

When your baby starts to learn pivoting you can often see them rocking on their stomach. At about 4 months your baby starts 'swimming' while on their stomach. His or her arms and legs are lifted up, kicking and making swimming motions. This activity may be accompanied by grumpy noises because learning a new skill is hard.

This is a normal developmental pattern at 4 and 5 months. No need to worry when the baby alternates swimming motions in a prone position with propping up on their elbows or wrists. However, if the baby does not switch from swimming motions to propping up on hands, contact your GP because your baby's neck and core extensor muscles as well as the chest muscles may be too weak, which may make it difficult for the baby to learn important motor skills.

Tips for parents:

💜 Put your baby in the prone position; place interesting objects on both sides to encourage the baby to pivot around their axis. Make sure the baby pivots both to the right and to the left.

💜 The baby should be on their stomach most of the time he or she is awake.

Crawling

Crawling is a skill that most parents eagerly look forward to. Crawling makes babies more independent; they are able to get a toy that has moved out of their reach and, naturally, a crawling baby can get into a lot of mischief. Some children want to investigate what in the earth is in a flower pot; others want to take a closer look at a power socket. When your child is able to move on their stomach from point A to point B, it is high time to think about babyproofing your home. In no time, your little one will be walking and taking interest in objects higher up.

What exactly is crawling? For us professionals, crawling is defined as a form of prone progression in which the tummy is on the floor. This is called the belly crawl. Belly crawl is different from the classic hands-and-knees crawl or cross crawl. There is no reason to worry – your child is not expected to do the hands-and-knees crawl at six or seven months old. They will learn that important skill later.

Infants use many different crawling styles. Some infants pull their body forward while the legs are passive. Some demonstrate a reciprocal crawling pattern, i.e. move one arm and the opposite knee forward at the same time. Others use only one side of their body. This is what happened to my son. He pushed himself forward with one leg only while using both hands alternatively. I did not let him use that convenient asymmetric movement for long. When I noticed that he wanted to move towards a toy, I lifted his right leg up for a moment and bent his left leg so that he would use that leg to push himself forward. He mastered alternating pulling with arms and pushing with legs. To correct patterns requires the constant presence of a parent and regular practise but it is worth it! Exercising both sides of the body symmetrically makes it easier for an infant to learn to crawl on their hands and knees. You have probably noticed that some children crawl backward. These 'reversers' often have stronger shoulder muscles compared with their lower body. The baby pushes with the arms instead of pulls, which has the unintended consequence of sending the baby backward if the surface is smooth enough. This may cause frustration because instead of moving closer to a toy in front of him or her, the baby is moving away from it. 'Reversers', too, can refine their skills to such a level that they can get to the desired object even when moving backwards. However, the cross crawl is when the baby bears weight on their hands and knees, then moves one arm and the opposite knee forward at the same time.

If there are anomalies in your child's crawling style it is important to train both their right and left sides equally to enable them to start crawling on their hands and knees. The cerebral hemispheres cooperate to ensure the development of physical coordination. The hands-and-knees crawl strengthens the baby's core and shoulder girdle, preparing their body for learning subsequent important motor skills.

Tips for parents:

💜 Place an interesting toy in front of your baby, just out of their reach to encourage moving forward.

💜 Learning to crawl may upset your baby because he or she is eager to move but their body is not cooperating yet. Help your baby to bend their legs and push forward.

💜 Make sure that your baby is using both sides of their body. If they want to push forward with one leg only, try to activate the other leg yourself. If your baby is pulling forward by using only their arms, push their legs down one by one to activate the baby's lower body and involve their legs in crawling.

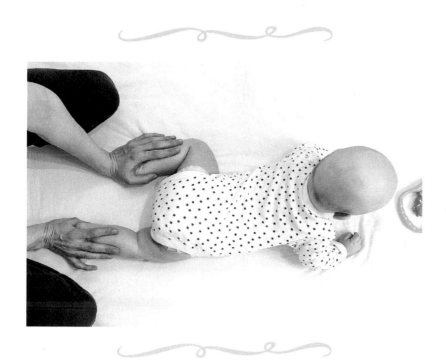

Activities
3-6 months

💜 Practise rolling from back to stomach
💜 Practise propping up on wrists in the prone position
💜 Practise pivoting on stomach
💜 Practise belly crawling

☆ ☆ ☆ ☆ ☆

Practise rolling from back to stomach:

1.

> **1.** Take your baby's legs into your hands and show him or her their toes. Put the baby's toes into their hands. You can put a toy on the baby's legs to encourage the baby to touch their toes.

2.

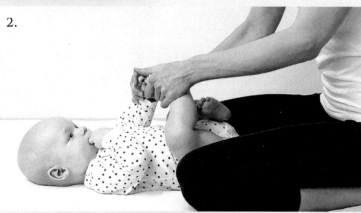

3.

1.

Note!

Practise rolling symmetrically on the right and left sides. This will make both sides equally strong.

2. Rest your baby on their back on the blanket. Hold your baby's thighs in your hands and bend their legs from the hip. Turn the baby on their right side so that their right leg is straight and left leg is bent. 'Walk' your fingers up under the baby's back to encourage him or her to complete the rolling motion. Repeat on other side.

2.

3.

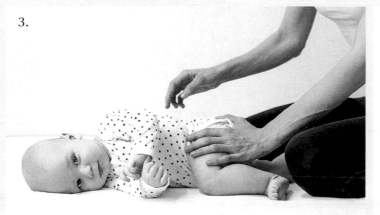

4.

1.

2.

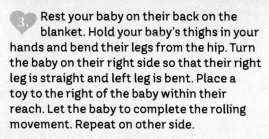

3.

4.

3. Rest your baby on their back on the blanket. Hold your baby's thighs in your hands and bend their legs from the hip. Turn the baby on their right side so that their right leg is straight and left leg is bent. Place a toy to the right of the baby within their reach. Let the baby to complete the rolling movement. Repeat on other side.

1.  2.

4. Rest your baby on their back on the blanket. Hold your baby's left arm and turn him or her on their right side. Let the baby complete the rolling movement. Repeat on other side.

3. 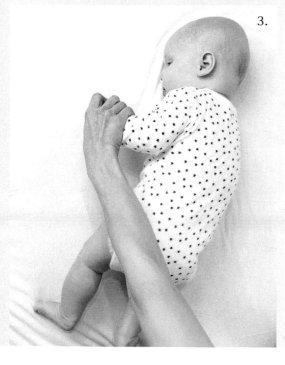 4.

Practise propping up on wrists in the prone position:

1. The baby is on their stomach. Use a toy to entice your baby to look up and stretch their core while supporting on wrists.

2. The baby is on their stomach. Roll up a towel and place it under the baby's armpits. Make sure the baby is supporting on their wrists.

Learning to pivot on stomach:

1. The baby is propped up on forearms in the prone position. Hold your baby's upper arms and lean him or her to the right, hold the position for a couple of seconds; repeat with other side.

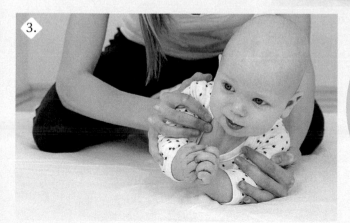

Tip!

Use the same exercise to teach your baby the crawling movement. Hold him or her on their side for longer and wait for him or her to bend their leg. Repeat the exercise with the other side of the baby's body.

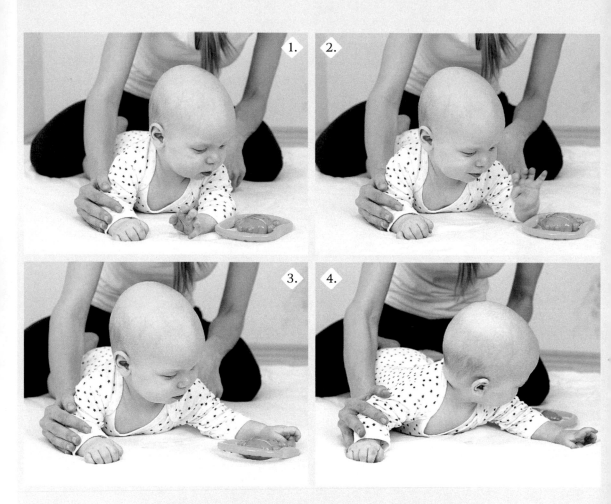

2. The baby is on their stomach. Place a toy to the left of your baby and encourage him or her to pivot around their axis. You can support their right hand. After the baby has moved to the left, place the toy further away from him or her and repeat the exercise. Repeat on other side.

1.

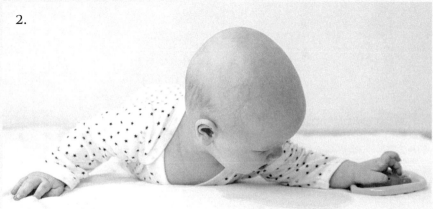

3. The baby is on their stomach. Place a toy next to the child's left arm. Wait for the baby to grab the toy and then move it further away. Repeat with the right side.

2.

3.

1.

4. Put your baby on their stomach on the exercise ball. Hold your baby's thighs so that your index fingers are on the baby's buttocks. Move slowly to the right and to the left in circles.

2.

3.

Practise belly crawling:

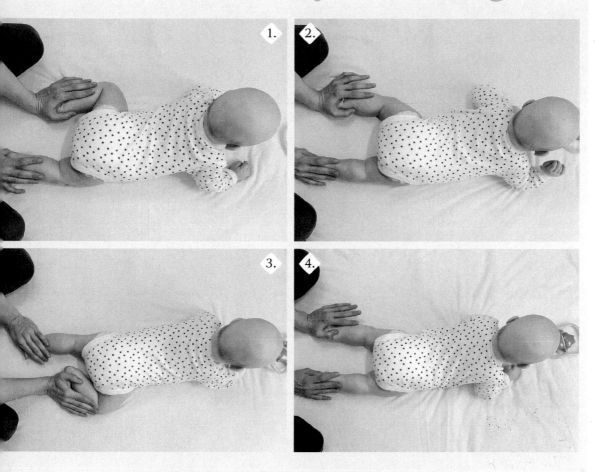

Place an interesting toy in front of your baby, just out of their reach. Bend the baby's left leg from the knee and place your hands under their soles so that the big toe and the innermost part of the sole are against your hand. Let the baby to extend his or her left leg. Repeat with the other side of the baby's body.

1.

2.

2. Place an interesting toy in front of your baby, just out of their reach. Bend the baby's leg from the knee. Make sure that the big toe and the innermost part of the sole are against your hand. Put your other hand under the baby's left arm-pit. Lean the baby slightly towards their bent leg (to the right) and let him or her extend their leg independently. Repeat with the other side of the baby's body.

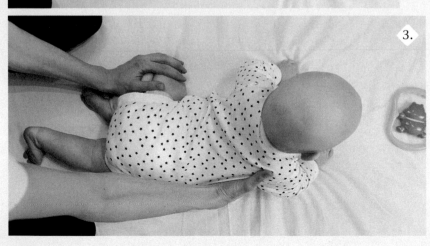

3.

"Sometimes the smallest
things take up the most
room in your heart."

6–9 months

Important motor skill milestones:

6 months on average – supporting on hands in the prone position:
your baby is supporting on hands in the prone position; their palms
are open.

7 to 8 months on average – keeping balance while seated:
your baby is able to keep their balance for a short time while seated.
Your baby has developed defensive reflexes that prevent him or her from
falling forward or sideward. He or she may still fall backward because they
are not able to extend their arm posteriorly to prevent falling backward.

**8 months on average – classic hands-and-knees crawl or cross
crawl:**
your baby is able to move from a seated position to their hands and knees,
rock him or herself and/or move forward on their hands and knees.

8 to 9 months on average – moving into and out of the sitting position:
your baby is able to independently get into the sitting position from
hands and knees or push themselves up into the sitting position
from lying on their side. Your baby can get down from the sitting
position on their hands and knees independently.

Propping up on hands in the prone position

At about 6 months your baby will start doing 'push-ups' while on their stomach. He or she will push up onto straight hands and fall back on their wrists. This may sometimes even make the baby a little cranky. There is no need to be alarmed – your baby would like to do more but their body is not very cooperative. Soon, they will master a new skill that enables him or her to investigate interesting objects that are placed higher. Propping up on hands is a prerequisite for getting up on hands and knees. Some children master these skills very quickly so that it seems that they skipped the propping up on hands phase and got immediately on their hands and knees.

Others need more time to get from propping up on hands in the prone position to rising up on hands and knees. But everything in its own time – babies develop at different rates. While your baby is actively practicing propping up on their wrists, he or she may start moving backward, especially if the surface (e.g. a slippery parquet floor) favours it. The baby pushes with arms instead of pulls, which send him or her backward. If the baby tries again and again, he or she may develop impressionable reversing skills.

At first, moving backward can frustrate the baby because they wanted to move forward. However, 'reversers' can become adept in the art of manoeuvring and are able to get to their desired toys.

Tips for parents:

- ♥ Use a toy to entice your baby to look up – this makes him or her to stretch their back and push up from the ground.

- ♥ Make sure that your baby is on their stomach most of their awake time.

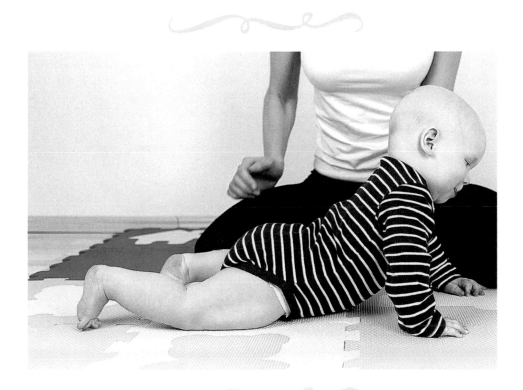

Getting on hands and knees and crawling on hands and knees

At about seven or eight months, after your infant has learned to prop up on hands, he or she will start trying to bend their knees and draw their legs under their belly. This process may take weeks and the baby's attempts to get up on his or her hands and knees often end in failure. This is because his or her muscles are too weak. But the purpose of this exercise is to strengthen their muscles. Getting on hands and knees may be hindered by a slippery floor or the baby's tights/leggings, which prevent them from maintaining the position even if he or she manages to get on all fours. You should pay attention to such seemingly unimportant small details in order to support your child in learning an important new skill. After your baby has mastered the skill of getting on all fours and can maintain that position for a short period of time, he or she will start learning how to shift their body weight. He or she rocks back and forth on hands and knees. That way the baby is repetitively shifting weight back and forth from the hands to the knees. Rocking helps to learn how to shift body weight in this new position.

This is a very important skill because the baby's weight will be on one hand and the opposite knee and he or she will have to shift weight in order to lift their limbs and move forward. This is why babies rock. This is an activity you can do together with your baby by showing how to rock forth and back. After your baby has learned to maintain his or her position on all fours and shift their body weight, they will want to move forward. First attempts often end with crashing on the belly because an infant's legs and arms are not strong enough to carry their body weight. Repeating the movement will strengthen the muscles and eventually, the child is able to carry their body weight on one hand and one leg. At seven to nine months, your baby has mastered a new style of moving – cross crawl – which is very important in terms of development. Cross crawl is a motor milestone that all children should attain. Parents should encourage their little ones to crawl on all fours, at least for a brief period of time. Cross crawl strengthens the muscles of the neck, shoulder girdle, core and limbs. These muscles are essential to prepare the baby for the skills that require huge effort, such as pulling up on furniture, maintaining balance while standing and walking independently.

Cross crawl has an important role in the development of spinal alignment. At birth, babies are in a state of flexion, still curled up, with their spine in a natural long c-shaped (convex) curve, just like it was inside the womb. As your baby's muscles and bones become stronger, she will slowly develop the characteristic S-shaped spine that adults have. As the neck muscles become stronger and head control improves a secondary curve (cervical lordosis) develops in the cervical region.

Therefore, it is very important to start putting your baby on their tummy as early as possible. Tummy time strengthens the baby's neck and core muscles, which are necessary for his or her spine to form lordosis curves.

The next physiological change is the formation of thoracic curvature or thoracic kyphosis. Thoracic kyphosis forms when the baby starts to belly crawl and cross crawl. Learning to maintain balance while seated also affects the formation of thoracic kyphosis. However, cross crawling plays a particularly crucial role in the formation of thoracic kyphosis. Cross crawl strengthens the muscles of the shoulder girdle, core and limbs. Strong muscles of the shoulder girdle and upper back contribute to the formation of thoracic kyphosis. If the baby does not crawl on their hands and knees, he or she may develop a flat back. This means that the thoracic curvature is insufficient and the back remains flat. A flat back may cause back pains later in life because the child's posture is underdeveloped and the shock of impact on joints and back while walking is not dampened sufficiently. Underdeveloped thoracic kyphosis may also affect the child's lung capacity because there is not enough space in the thorax for the lungs to expand to full capacity.

A second physiological curvature or lumbar lordosis forms when the muscles that help to maintain balance while standing and walking become stronger. If the child tries to pull him or herself up on furniture too soon or, worse still, if parents start to put their baby on their feet before they are ready for it, the baby misses the cross crawl phase and the muscles of their shoulder girdle and upper back fail to become strong enough for the formation of thoracic kyphosis. Therefore, the baby should have enough time and opportunity to belly crawl and cross crawl before graduating to standing and walking, which require enormous effort.

Strong muscles contribute to the development of the physiological structures of the spine and the balance reactions of the core. Cross crawling plays an important role in the development of coordination. Cross crawl – moving by alternating arms and legs – activates the right and left hemispheres of the brain in a balanced way, which creates conditions for performing other activities that require balance (including walking, running, etc.). The child can practise an activity that is very similar to walking (when we walk we also alternate the use of limbs).

Children are smart and will find a way to learn that important skill. We all want our children to be active and moving around. Let your baby develop at their own rate. Do not deprive your baby the possibility to learn an important skill that is essential for the development of the spine and core muscles.

Tips for parents:

💜 Start putting your child on their tummy early on! Being in the prone position strengthens the neck, core and shoulder girdle muscles. These groups of muscles are essential for learning motor skills, such as rolling, belly crawling, cross crawling, etc.

💜 Do not keep your baby in a forced position (bouncer, car seat, sling, etc.) for extended periods! Babies need to move to learn motor skills. A child that is in a bouncy seat for a long time may become lazy because he or she cannot develop the skills of rolling, crawling and moving on hands and knees. A major factor contributing towards crawling and moving on hands and knees is being in the prone position on a play mat or blanket.

💜 Do not stand your baby up before they can do it him or herself by pulling up on a support! Otherwise the muscle tone of their legs may increase, making it difficult to bend their legs (as crawling requires bending legs, it will make it difficult for the child to learn to crawl).

💜 Do not use a baby walker or door bouncer or any other standing aid! If a baby is stood up before he or she can pull themselves up on a support, the muscle tone of their legs may increase. Increased muscle tone makes learning to belly crawl and cross crawl very difficult for the child.

💜 Standing the baby up too soon or using standing aids may have an adverse effect on the formation of physiological curvatures of the baby's spine.

Keeping balance while seated and moving in and out of sitting independently

When can I put my baby into a sitting position? This is one of the questions most frequently asked of me. My answer is always the same: a baby can sit for an extended period of time when he or she is capable of getting into a sitting position from lying on their side or from a four-point position (from all fours). This usually happens at seven to nine months; some children do it earlier, others later.

At three to five months, all children start to actively stretch forward. First, they do it from a semi-reclined position. As the baby's muscles become stronger, he or she is able to lift their head while lying on a flat surface (floor, bed, etc.). It may be difficult to hold your baby on your lap in a semi-reclined position because it seems that he or she is trying to get into sitting position. Parents often misinterpret such behaviour. They assume that their baby wants to sit up while the little one has a different objective – to train their core muscles in preparation for rolling over.

In the first year children do not get into the sitting position this way; instead, they sit up from lying on their side or from all fours. Between three and five months of age, it is too early to put your baby into the sitting position because their core muscles are too weak for such effort and do not support their spine sufficiently.

A newborn's bones and spine are very soft and malleable. They have not developed the strength in their muscles and bones to hold the position so they collapse into a rounded back. If the abnormal curvature of the back is encouraged every day, the baby's spine will develop along with the curvature and the baby may develop a hunchback (a hump on the back). Sitting a baby up too early may have an adverse effect on the spine development and cause back pains and posture problems later in life.

If you put your baby in a sitting position often he or she will eventually agree with it, even if it seems clumsy and uncomfortable. Babies are curious and it is much easier to observe the world while sitting up, rather than being in prone or supine positions. If the baby has never experienced sitting, they will not miss it and will sit up when they and their body are ready to do this.

All children are different. Therefore, let your child develop at their own pace, just like their body is programmed to develop. If you start putting your baby in the sitting position early, they

will get used to sitting. If the baby is used to sitting, they may skip important motor milestones, such as rolling over, belly crawling and crawling on hands and knees. Let your child discover sitting independently – he or she will be more confident and able to take their own abilities into account.

Children who started sitting up early may enjoy sitting but they are not able to push themselves up into the sitting position because they had no possibility to master the necessary skills. Neither will they be able to move out of sitting when they get tired. If a child with weak core muscles tries to move out of sitting, he or she can hardly do it without falling over. This may damage the baby's confidence and sense of security.

If a child can practise getting into and out of the sitting position and is not forced to sit up, they will be much more confident when moving from one position to another and will fall less often because they can take into account their physical capabilities and is able to choose in which position he or she prefers to play. He or she can also stretch out their arm to avoid falling. Naturally, not everything works at first attempt but the baby will develop parachute reactions in the course of learning and trying.

Parachute reactions (putting a hand down to prevent falling over) first develop in the forward direction. Babies can prevent falling over by extending their arms at six months already. At seven and eight months, your baby can extend an arm to prevent falling sideways (lateral parachutes). Finally the posterior parachute emerges at approximately nine months, when the child extends the arms posteriorly to prevent falling backward.

At seven or eight months, your baby is able to keep their balance for a short time while seated. If your baby cannot move into and out of the sitting position, he or she is not ready to sit up for an extended period of time. Naturally, you can put the baby into a highchair at meal times to eat solid food. Sitting on mummy's or daddy's lap does not do any harm either. In those positions the baby is able to rest when their core muscles get tired. However, if you are planning to play with your baby on the floor while the baby is sitting up, teach him or her how to move into and out of the sitting position independently. Do not make your baby to sit up for an extended period of time.

Practicing sitting balance could go hand in hand with teaching the baby how to move into and out of the sitting position. Children learn how to move into and out of the sitting position at about 8 to 9 months on average. My son started to move into the sitting position a few weeks after turning seven months old. A little earlier than the average but, as I said, each child develops at their own pace – it probably was the right time for him. I believe that one reason why he was able to sit up so early was that he first started to move into the sitting position from lying on his side. Later, when he mastered getting on all fours, he started to push himself into the sitting position from that position.

It is important to make sure that the baby moves into and out of the sitting position from both sides. I recall that at first my son moved into the sitting position from his left side but in a week he had already learned to sit up from his right side. If you notice that your baby starts to move into the sitting position from one side, try to entice him or her to also do this from the other side. This will train the muscles of both sides equally and prevents muscle imbalances.

Tips for parents:

💜 Do not put your child into the sitting position or use sitting aids before he or she has shown interest in sitting. Note! Stretching forward is not an indication that the baby wants to sit up. Otherwise the baby may miss important milestones in their motor development. Early sitting may have an adverse effect on spine development.

💜 Practicing sitting balance could go hand in hand with teaching the baby how to move into and out of the sitting position.

💜 Do not force your child to sit; let them discover the position by him or herself. This will prevent the child from falling over when moving into and out of the sitting position. The baby can take into account their physical capabilities and can extend their arm to prevent falling.

💜 Make sure that your child uses both sides when moving into and out of sitting position.

Activities
6–9 months

- 💜 Practise propping up on hands in the prone position
- 💜 Practise getting on hands and knees
- 💜 Practise cross crawling
- 💜 Practise moving into and out of the sitting position
- 💜 Practise maintaining balance while seated

Practise propping up on hands in the prone position:

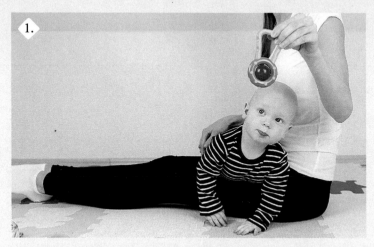

Place your baby on your lap so that their hands reach the floor. Show him or her a toy to entice them to look up and lift their right arm to grasp the toy. Repeat with the left hand.

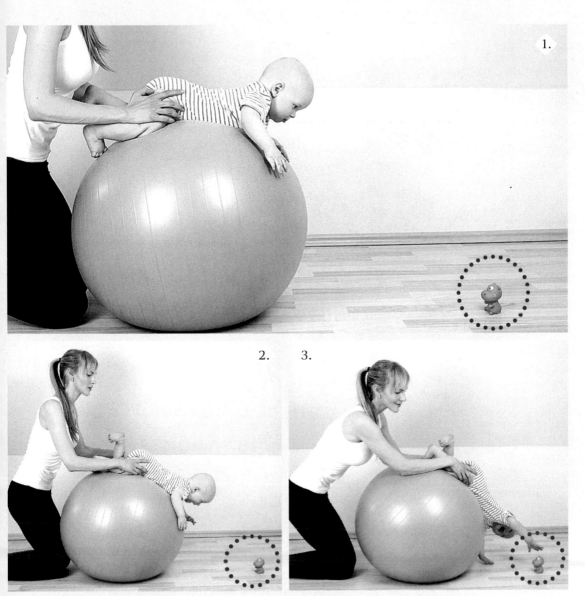

1.

2.   3.

Put your baby on an exercise ball in the prone position. Place a toy on the floor in front of the baby. Move the ball forward and let your baby put their hands on the floor and to grab the toy.

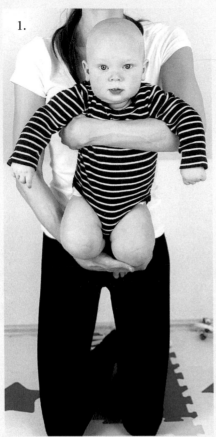

1.

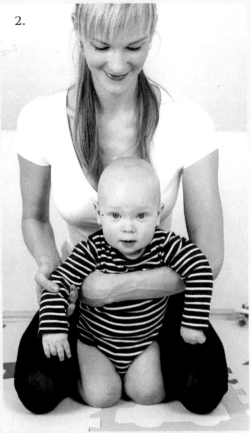

2.

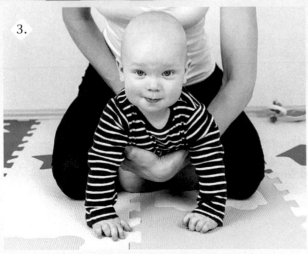

3.

2. Put your baby on your lap. Bend the baby's legs from the knee. Put the child on their knees between your legs. Entice him or her to put their hands down. When the baby is steadily on all fours rock him or her back and forth.

1.

2.

3. If your baby has mastered belly crawling entice him or her to push him or herself up on a support. Let him or her crawl across your legs so that the baby moves onto their hands and knees.

3.

Tip!

Entice your baby to crawl on a diaper pack. A diaper pack is a safe support of suitable height – an excellent tool to practise standing on hands and knees.

Practise cross crawling:

1. Place an interesting toy in front of your baby, just out of their reach. Hold your baby's thighs in your hands and move their legs forward one after another. When the baby starts to move toward the toy, do not let him or her get back on their stomach immediately.

2.

3.

Tip!

You can use a scarf or a piece of material to practise cross crawl. Put a scarf underneath your baby. Lift the baby slightly up to make it easier to lighten the weight on their hands and knees. Help him or her to move towards a toy.

Practise moving into and out of the sitting position:

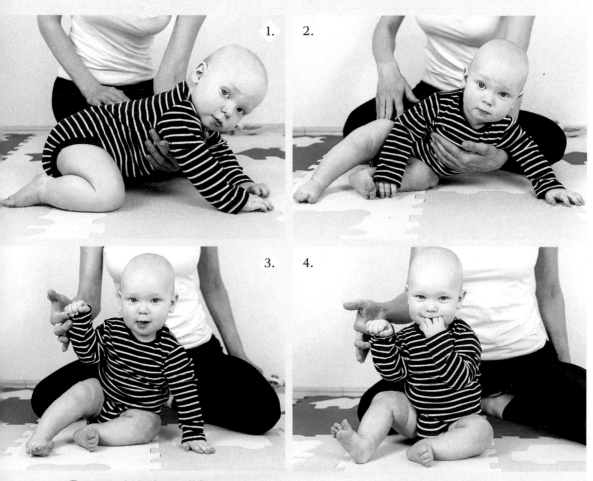

1.   2.

3.   4.

💙 Your baby is on all fours sideways to you. Put your hand on your baby's chest and push their body weight back. Roll the baby over their left hip into the sitting position. Let the baby push him or herself into the sitting position or help by holding their right arm. Repeat with the other side.

2. Rest your baby on their back on the blanket. Put your hand on the baby's left thigh and hold their right hand with your left. Roll the baby on their left side and let him or her push into the sitting position themselves. Repeat with the other side.

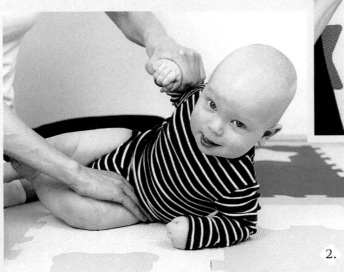

1.

2.

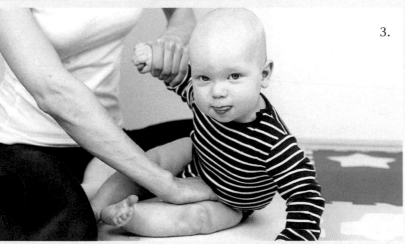

3.

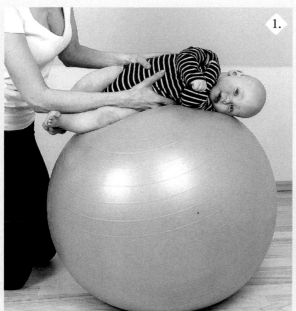

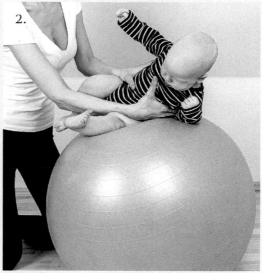

3. Put your baby on an exercise ball on their back. Hold your baby's trunk. Move the ball forward and roll the baby on their left side. Move the ball slowly towards yourself and let the baby push into the sitting position themselves. Repeat with the other side.

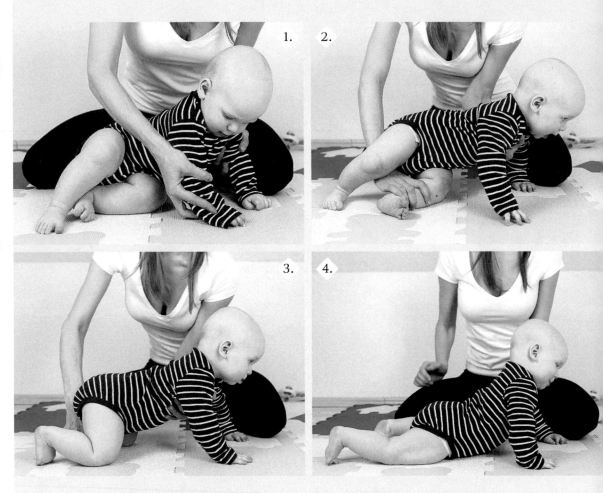

4. The baby is in front of you in a sitting position. Put the baby's left hand on the floor with the baby supporting on their hand. Put the baby's right hand next to their left hand so that the baby is now supporting on both hands. Hold your baby's left leg and roll the baby over into the sitting position or let him or her lower themselves down on their belly. Repeat with the other side.

Practise maintaining balance while seated:

1.

1. The baby is in front of you in a sitting position. Show your baby a toy, holding the toy high, and entice them to lift their hand and reach towards the toy. Repeat with both sides of the baby's body.

2.

Tip!

Let your baby extend their arm forward and backward to grasp a toy.

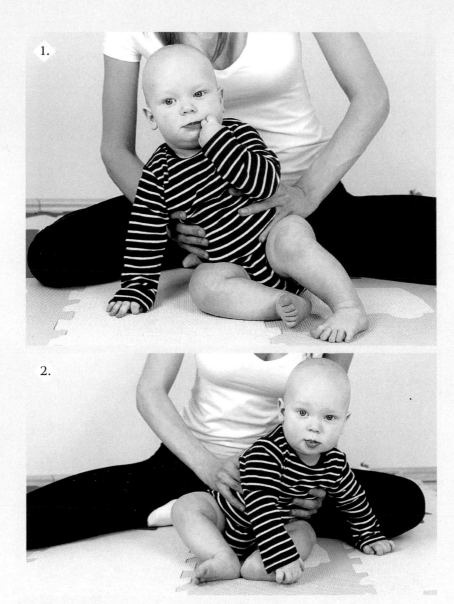

1.

2.

2. The baby is in front of you in a sitting position. Hold your baby's trunk and tilt him or her slowly to the right and to the left so that the baby can put their hand on the floor.

1.

2.

3.

4.

3. The baby is on the exercise ball in a sitting position. Move the ball slowly back and forth and circle the ball both to the right and to the left.

9 months
to the first
steps

Important motor skill milestones:

8 to 9 months on average – pulling to stand:
your baby can pull him or herself on their knees while supporting
on furniture, put their foot down and push themselves up.

**9 to 10 months on average – moving from standing into squat,
semi-kneeling and sitting positions:**
your baby is able to get down from a standing position by him or herself
while holding on to a support. Your baby moves from standing into squat,
semi-kneeling or sitting positions.

9 to 10 months on average – cruising:
your baby starts stepping sideways while holding onto a piece of furniture.

11 to 12 months on average – walking with or without support:
your baby starts walking with support. Many children find
it helpful to push a pouffe or another object in front of
them as they begin to walk. After practicing walking
with support your baby will soon be able to walk unaided.

Pulling to stand and getting back down from standing

Getting on their feet is a very important developmental milestone for your baby. It is also an important milestone for parents because it seems that life is getting easier now that they don't have to carry their baby around. Seasoned parents know that this is simply not true.

Now is the time when very dangerous situations may occur. The baby wants to investigate all those interesting objects that have been out of their reach so far. This means that the baby can pull an object from the table or shelf down onto him or herself. The first attempts to pull themselves up are rather wobbly. Parents should bear in mind that their child is going to fall over a lot because their body is not able to respond adequately to their wishes.

As a physical therapist, I do not recommend trying to intercept every single fall. Neither do I recommend using a baby helmet to soften falls. Using a helmet affects the child's ability to develop risk awareness. When the child falls on their back and hits their head repeatedly, he or she will learn to protect their head by drawing their chin to their chest. If you use a helmet the child is not aware of the danger and cannot protect their head when the helmet is removed.

The first attempts at balance holding should be supervised by a parent to make sure that the child does not hurt themselves. Parents should be particularly attentive about sharp corners, stone floors and other dangerous objects. Pulling up while holding onto a support and falling down is a necessary process – the child will become aware of their ability to maintain balance.

To make the process easier for your child you should teach him or her how to get down from a standing position. Children usually get down into squat, semi-kneeling or sitting positions. In order to teach a child how to get down from a standing position, parents make sure that the child masters at least one of the above three methods. The baby becomes more independent and does not get in danger when you turn your back to him or her.

Parents should not react to each whimper and pick their child up because children learn through repetition. If you have saved your child ten times and lift him or her up when they get in trouble, they will get the impression that this is the solution for each difficult situation. The child pulls him or herself up while holding onto a support, gets tired and starts complaining and mummy and daddy hurry to help. This will make your child dependent on you because they have not had an opportunity to deal with a new situation or you have not been able to direct them to find a solution him or herself.

When your child is ready to stand up, they will pull themselves up from the semi-kneeling position. He or she gets on their knees beside a support, holds onto it and puts the sole of one foot down. They then push themselves up on that foot and put the sole of the other foot down. Just the same way you get up from kneeling position.

Some babies can get vertical by pulling with their hands and extending their legs. The child is on their knees next to a support and holds onto it but mainly uses their hands to pull themselves up and extends both legs at the same time. This movement pattern is usually used by children who are not quite ready to stand up while holding onto a support. The have the desire but not enough muscle strength in their legs and core to do it the right way.

If your child wants to pull him or herself up by using only hands, remove any low objects onto which he or she likes to support themselves and let them strengthen their leg and core muscles by belly crawling or cross crawling. If he or she still finds ways to pull themselves up, you need to retrain your baby to get up from the semi-kneeling position. Getting into the standing position from the semi-kneeling position strengthens your baby's legs because they have to push up from the ground. It is also to make sure that the child uses both sides of their body symmetrically, i.e. alternatively uses both legs to push themselves up. Getting into the standing position from the semi-kneeling position is necessary for the child to learn shifting their body weight while standing. This skill is a precondition for walking.

Parents eagerly await the day when their baby is ready to stand up and sometimes they start putting their baby on their feet long before the child is ready to discover that position. Various standing aids, such as a baby walker or a door bouncer, are also very popular. Parents start putting their child in standing aids long before the child develops an interest in pulling themselves up into a standing position.

Putting your child on their feet or using standing aids may have serious consequences that hinder the normal development of motor skills. If you start putting your child in a baby walker or door bouncer before the child has shown interest in standing up and has not trained his or her leg muscles by belly crawling and cross crawling, the muscle tone of their legs may increase. This may lead to the child skipping important stages of motor development, such as belly crawling and cross crawling. To perform these activities the child needs to bend their legs. If their extensor muscles are stiff, learning the movements required for crawling may be very difficult. Once you introduce your baby to the standing position they may not be longer interested in being and moving on their belly or on all fours. This means that the child is skipping important stages of motor development. Your child may also start standing up by extending their legs because it is difficult for him or her to bend their leg and put their foot down to get up from a semi-kneeling position. The child's walking pattern may be distorted because it is easier for the child to stand and walk on tiptoes due to tension in the leg muscles. If standing and walking on tiptoes continues, the muscles tighten and the Achilles tendon shortens, which makes it very difficult for the child to put their feet flat on the floor.

It may seem that if you keep standing your baby on their feet, their muscles will strengthen and he or she will master walking faster, but actually it may delay walking because the child's core muscles are not strong enough for the child to maintain balance while standing.

When the child is confined in a baby walker he or she may get the impression that standing and walking is easy. However, when he or she is eventually taken out of the walker, the baby has no sense of balance and no awareness of danger. His or her core muscles are not used to working to maintain balance and are weak, and the baby will tumble a lot.

You should also bear in mind that baby walkers are considered to be very dangerous because babies can fall and get seriously hurt. Especially when they move from bare floorboards onto a carpet. A baby moving around in a baby walker may also pull objects from the table or shelf down onto themselves because parents assume that their baby is confined in a safe place and nothing bad can happen to them. Remember, it is best for your baby to discover the standing position by his or herself. This way their body is completely ready for the effort and there will be fewer problems with achieving other important motor development milestones.

Tips for parents:

♥ Avoid putting your baby on their feet too often. The muscle tone of their feet may increase, which may lead to the child skipping important motor development milestones.

♥ Do not use standing aids (baby walker or door bouncer). These tools may be dangerous and have an adverse effect on your child's normal motor development.

♥ Make sure the baby uses alternatively both legs to push him or herself up.

♥ If your child prefers to get up by pulling him or herself up with their hands and extending their legs, teach them to stand up from a semi-kneeling position. Remember to train getting up from both legs.

♥ Let your baby try to get down from standing independently – under your supervision, of course. If your child does not know how to get down safely, teach them to squat, move into a semi-kneeling position or to plop on their bottom.

Cruising, keeping balance while standing and walking

Within a few weeks of learning to pull themselves to a standing position, your baby will take interest in shuffling along in this new position. Many parents assume that once their baby is pulling themselves up while holding onto a support it is time to practise walking. Do not forget a very important intermediate phase – cruising, i.e. stepping sideways while holding onto a piece of furniture. Cruising is a safe way to practise stepping movements and shifting body weight, to practise standing balance and to strengthen core, hip and leg muscles.

Make sure that your baby is cruising in both directions. Otherwise one side of their body is used more, which may lead to muscle imbalance. If your baby is able to step sideways only in one direction, motivate them to cruise in the opposite direction to make sure that both sides of their body are used equally.

Sometimes babies only cruise in one direction because of how pieces of furniture are positioned in the room. For example, the baby pulls him or herself up from their usual place and can move only in one direction. Rearranging furniture helps the child to learn to cruise in both directions.

When your baby has mastered cruising while holding onto a piece of furniture he or she will start to look for opportunities to train keeping their balance. He or she lets go of furniture and tries to stand without support. During this phase they may tumble a lot. However, this learning process is necessary for your child to walk independently.

After trying to keep balance, your baby will start moving lighter items, which he or she has used as support. Your baby will start walking alone by pushing a stool, chair or a toy car in front of them. Many parents are keen to help their child walk. Walking the baby by holding their hands is very popular among parents. As a physical therapist, I do not recommend walking your baby. Parents believe that if they walk their baby, the baby will achieve walking faster. In reality, it can delay your baby's first steps. If you walk your baby, he or she is less aware of their surroundings and abilities. By holding your baby's hands, we do not focus on practicing the skills necessary for walking. If your baby is walked by holding their hands, they will get a false impression of their skills and ability to keep balance. And when you eventually want to let go of their hand, their core muscles will be too weak to maintain balance. When your child tries to walk alone, he or she will tumble, get hurt and want you to hold their hand again. He or she will remain dependent on you for a long time and mastering walking may take longer than expected. Children, who can

practise walking independently and at their own pace, develop a perception of how to do this safely. Through repeated trial and error, your child will learn how to plan ahead their movements and to maintain balance. The child will know their limits and tumble less.

If you start walking your baby they, very likely, will want to do it over and over. Before you notice, you will be walking your baby every day, throughout the day. By trying to help your baby you will teach them to walk with you holding their hands. Letting your child practise walking at their own pace will boost their confidence. He or she will feel that they have achieved something important without their parents' help.

We often fail to notice that we are pulling the child up while walking our baby. This means that the child is walking on tiptoes. Think about it – how do you walk? You put your heel down first, followed by your toe. Walking your child may distort their walking pattern, which may lead to health problems later in life.

In order to walk your child you have to stoop down. As I said above, walking your baby by holding their hands may become an established habit. If you spend a quarter of your day stooping down you may develop back pain! If you have introduced your child to walking with you, he or she will be reluctant to give up such a fun activity.

It is better to let your child to practise walking on their own. If it seems that your child has few opportunities to practise walking, make him or her a walker that they can push in front of themselves. A cardboard box of suitable height, filled with heavy objects (such as books) to prevent it moving too fast, is an excellent choice. Walking by pushing a cardboard box is a relatively safe option for your baby. It does not move as fast as the wheeled baby walkers available at shops. It is also safer. If your baby tumbles and hits him or herself against the box he or she is less likely to get hurt than when hitting themselves against a baby walker made of plastic or wood. A cardboard box is also much more stable than many baby walkers available at shops. Use your imagination and creativity and make a cardboard 'walker' instead of damaging your back by walking your baby.

Do not assume that your baby will be walking in a few months after pulling themselves up against furniture. Each child develops at their own rate. Your baby's temperamental traits may influence how quickly they will learn to walk. More restrained and cautious children may start walking later than energetic and rambunctious kids that are not discouraged by tumbling over.

My son started to pull himself up against furniture very early. At seven and half months he discovered that he could stand while holding onto furniture and took his first steps alone a week before his first birthday. He graduated from cross crawling to walking at about 13 months. Thus, there were several months between standing and taking his first independent steps spent strengthening his core muscles and the muscles of his limbs by cross crawling and standing, and cruising while holding onto furniture.

Let your baby strengthen their core and limb muscles, and develop coordination and cooperation of the two hemispheres of their brain by practising belly crawling and cross crawling. Bear in mind the importance of the cross crawl in the development of the physiological curvatures of the spine. Your child has their whole life ahead to walk around!

Tips for parents:

♥ Everything starts from cruising. Let your baby step sideways to the right and to the left. Your baby will learn how to shift their body weight from one leg to another, practise maintaining balance and as their muscles become stronger, their hips and core will become more stable.

♥ Let your baby practise walking while holding a walker. Find a stable and safe object which your child can push in front of themselves. It can be a pouffe, a cardboard box or a toy crate with casters (make sure that the casters are not moving too quickly and that the support is safe for your baby).

♥ Do not walk your baby by holding their hands! By holding our baby's hands you are pulling him or her up and they walk on their tiptoes. This may distort your baby's walking pattern.

♥ Letting your child practise walking alone will boost their confidence. He or she will develop the skill of learning from their mistakes – the skill necessary to both succeed and cope with failures. The child will know their limits and tumble less often.

♥ Walking your child by holding their hands will make your child depend on you. Constant stooping may cause strain on your back and lead to back pain.

Activities
9 months to first steps

💜 Practise standing on full soles
💜 Practise pulling up while holding onto a support
💜 Practise getting down from standing
💜 Practise cruising
💜 Practise maintaining balance while standing
💜 Practise walking

Practise standing on full soles:

1.

Sit down on the floor. Sit your baby astride on your thigh. Hold your baby's leg and tilt them alternatively on each side so that they support on the sole of their feet. This exercise prepares your baby for becoming vertical. Practise supporting on full soles and shifting body weight from one leg to another.

2.

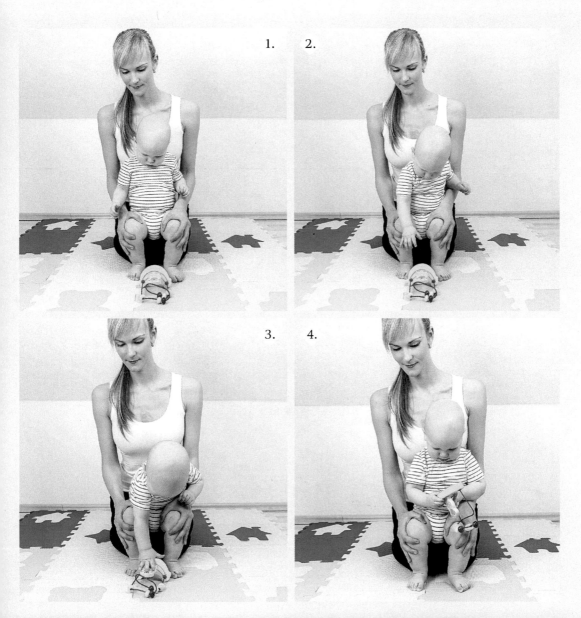

1.   2.

3.   4.

2. Get down on your knees. Put your baby on your knees so that their feet are supported on the floor. Place an interesting toy on the floor in front of the baby. Hold your baby's thighs and let your baby pick up the toy. This exercise will teach your child how to support their body weight with their feet and stand on full soles.

1.

3. Hold your baby's thighs in your hands and put him or her down in a squat position. Make sure the baby is supporting on their full soles. Rock slightly back and forth. This exercise will teach your child how to support their body weight with their feet and stand on full soles.

Practise pulling to stand:

 1. 2.

3.

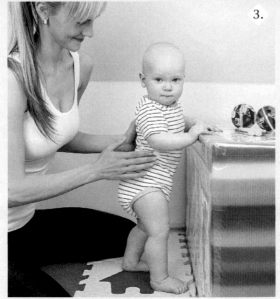

1. Entice your baby to get into the kneeling position while holding onto a support. Take your baby's right leg and put it down on the full sole. Shift the baby's body weight towards their right leg so that the baby can push to standing.

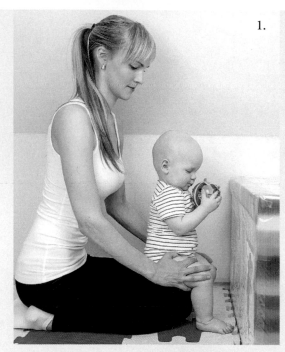

1.

2.

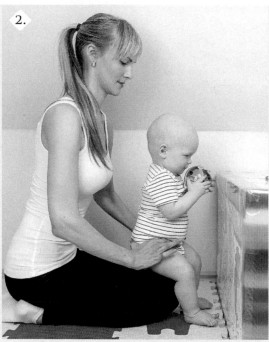

3.

2. Kneel down next to a piece of furniture and place your baby on your lap so that their feet are supported on the floor. Hold your baby's hips and encourage him or her to pull up against furniture.

3. Sit down with your legs extended. Sit your baby on your legs so that their legs are between your thighs. Use a toy to entice your baby to stand up independently.

Note!

Make sure the baby is supporting on their full soles.

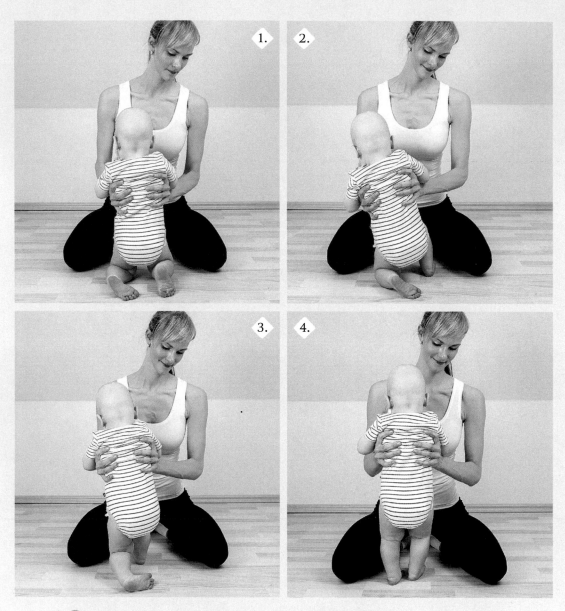

4. The following is a good way to pick your child up to teach them how to get up using the right movements. Put your hands under your baby's armpits and shift their body weight to their left side. The baby will put their right foot down on full sole. Then shift the baby's body weight to the right so that the baby can push themselves to standing. Repeat with the other side.

Practise getting down from standing:

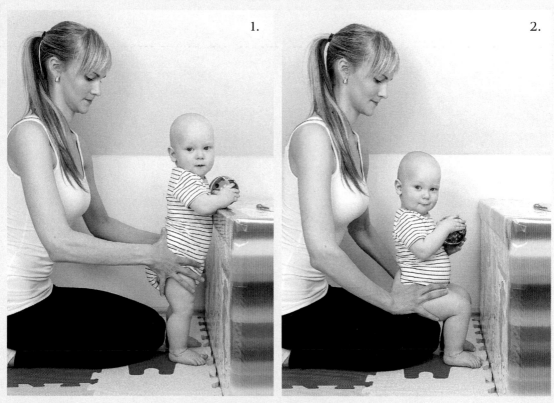

1.

2.

1. Kneel down behind your baby's back. Hold your baby's hips and encourage them to sit on your lap. Tell your baby to squat. When your baby has mastered squatting you can move further away from him or her and repeat the exercise so that the baby squats but does not sit on your lap.

2.

3.

2. Your baby is standing while holding onto a support. Use a toy to entice your child to put their hand down. The baby can squat safely by supporting themselves with their hand.

Practise stepping sideways:

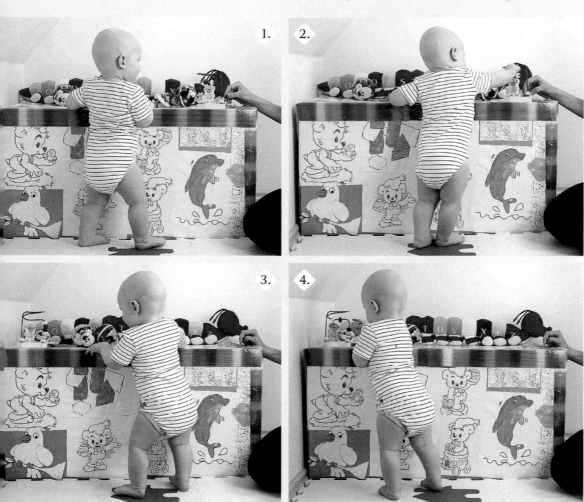

1.   2.

3.   4.

After your baby has mastered standing while holding onto furniture, it is time to teach him or her cruising. Use a toy to entice your baby to move sideways. Repeat the exercise to make sure the baby cruises in both directions.

Practise maintaining balance while standing:

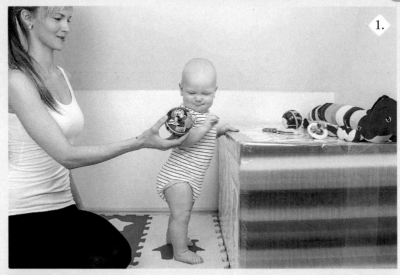

1.

2.

1. After your baby has mastered standing while holding onto furniture, hold a toy behind their back and encourage them to grab the toy. Repeat the exercise on both sides.

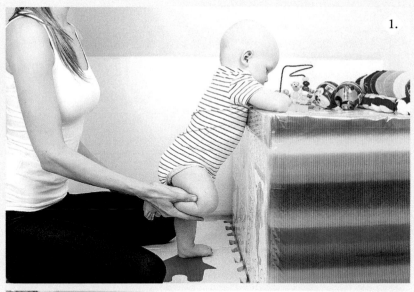

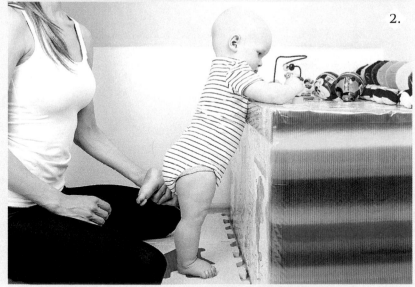

2.

Your baby is standing while holding onto a support.
Hold their right leg so that the baby is supporting
on their left leg. Repeat with the left leg.

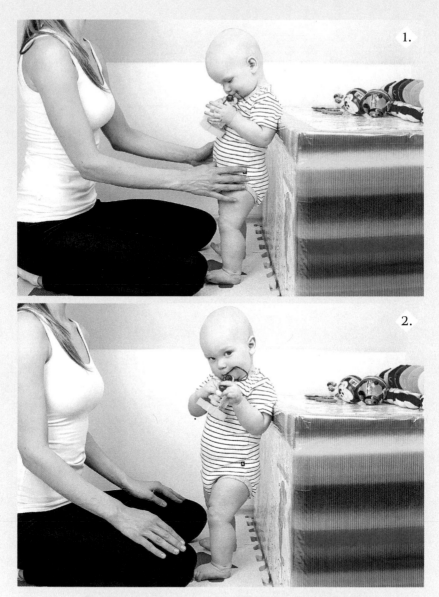

3. Give your baby an interesting toy and stand your baby up with their back against furniture. The baby will learn that he or she does not have to hold onto something in order to stand.

1.   2.

4. Give your baby an interesting toy and stand him or her in front of you. When the baby is standing firmly, let them go so that they can practise maintaining balance without support.

Practise walking:

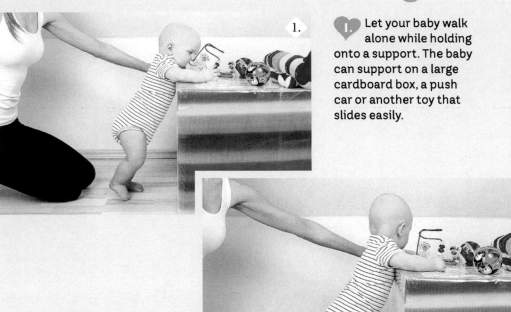

1. Let your baby walk alone while holding onto a support. The baby can support on a large cardboard box, a push car or another toy that slides easily.

Note!

If you are using a baby walker with wheels, make sure the wheels are not moving too fast! The baby should only use a walker under your supervision or on a carpet that slows down the movement of the wheels.

1. 2.

3.

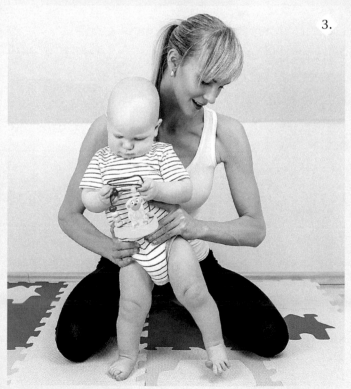

2. Hold your baby's hips to practise walking. Tilt the baby to the left to make him or her bring their right foot forward. Tilt the baby to the right to make him or her bring their left foot forward and take a step.

Holding the baby

During their first year, your little one needs to be close to you. Discovering the world is much more fun from the arms of mummy or daddy. Here are some recommendations for holding your baby without causing muscle tension in their back and putting strain on their spine. Remember to carry your baby on both sides of your body alternatively.

Holding the baby:

1. Place your baby with their back to your chest and their legs bent.

2. Put your right arm under the baby's right arm and bring it down under their left thigh. Keep their leg in the bent position. Alternate between your body sides to prevent asymmetry.

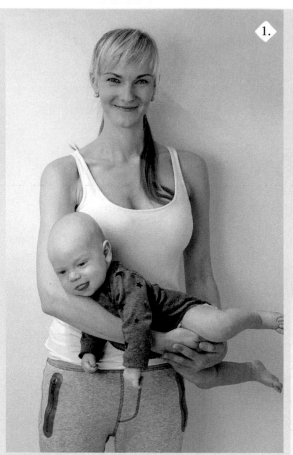

3. Put your baby on your arm in the prone position. Alternate between your left and right arm to prevent asymmetry.

4. Put your baby on your shoulder with their hands supporting on your shoulder. Alternate between your left and right shoulder to prevent asymmetry.

Having fun with mummy and daddy

These activities will make the time spent with your baby even more fun. Besides having fun, most activities will stimulate your baby's development. Exercising with your baby is also a great workout for mummy and daddy. As your baby grows, picking him or her up and holding them will become more difficult – just like replacing lighter dumbbells with heavier ones. These fun activities are suitable for babies starting from three months. At three months, the baby's neck muscles are strong enough for various lifting and dangling exercises.

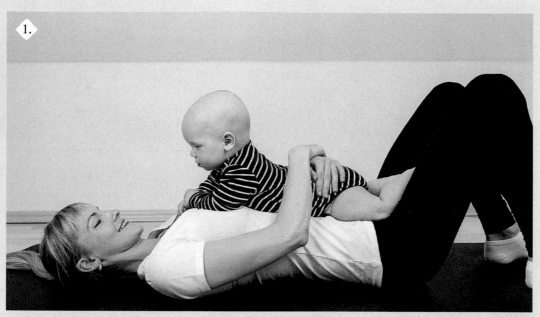

1.

2.

Supine position. Put your baby on your chest in the prone position.
Lift your hips slowly from the ground and bring them slowly down again.

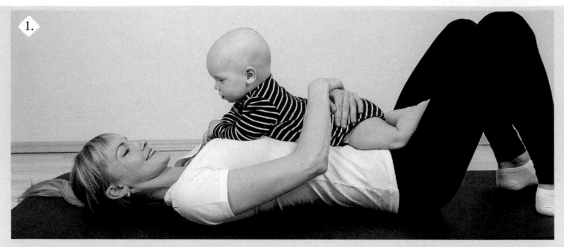

1.

2. Supine position. Put your baby on your chest in the prone position. Hold your baby's thighs in your hands and raise him or her above your face, kiss or touch their nose with yours. Lower the baby slowly back on your chest.

2.

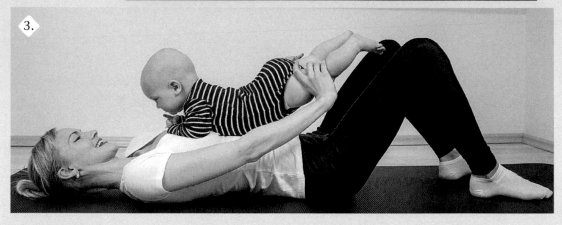

3.

3. Supine position. Put your baby on your chest in the supine position. Hold your baby's thighs in your hands and raise him or her above your face. Kiss your baby and lower your baby slowly back on your chest.

4. Supine position. Place your baby on your chest in the prone position. Hold your baby's body and lift him or her up above your face. Turn the baby left and right and lower your baby slowly back on your chest.

5. Supine position. Put your baby on your lap in a semi-reclined position. Support their body with one hand and put your other hand on the back of your head. Do sit-ups to strengthen your abs.

6. Supine position. Place your baby on your legs in the prone position. Put your thumbs in your baby's palms and grab their forearms. Bend and extend your knees.

1.

7. Supine position. Put your baby on your legs in the prone position. Put your thumbs in your baby's palms and grab their forearms. Sit up quickly and lower down on your back.

2.

3.

1.

2.

8. Supine position. Place your baby on your legs in the prone position. Hold. your baby's body and extend your legs from the knees.

9. Supine position. Put your baby on your legs. Put your thumbs in your baby's palms and grab their forearms. Lift your head and bring your legs towards your head.

10. Supine position. Put your baby on your legs. Hold your baby's legs and slowly lift him or her up. Put the baby on your chest.

1.

11. Sit down on the floor with your legs slightly bent. Hold your baby's body and move him or her to the right and to the left. If your child is not yet standing independently, do not put their feet down.

2.

3.

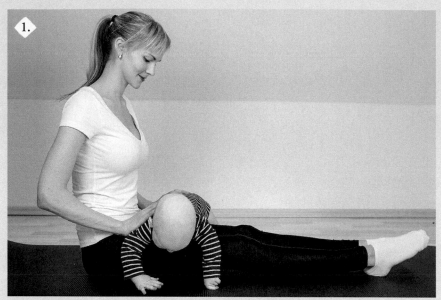

12. Sit down on the floor with your legs extended. Put your baby on your lap. Hold your baby by their shoulder and hip and roll him or her slowly along your legs to your toes. Hold your baby by their opposite shoulder and hip and roll them back to your lap.

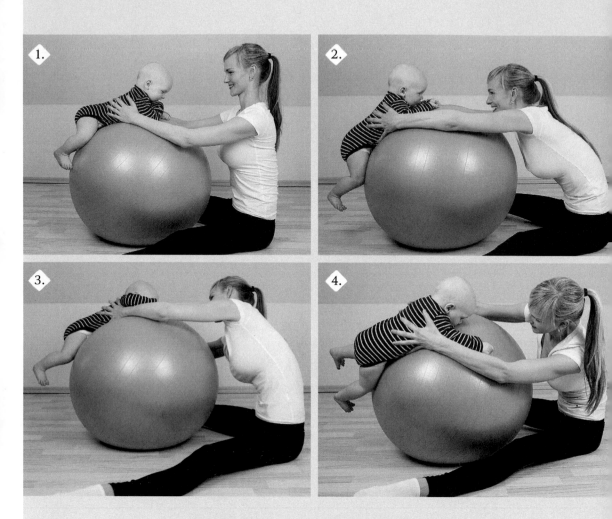

1.

2.

3.

4.

13. Place the exercise ball between your legs. Put your baby on the ball in the prone position facing you. Move the ball slowly back and forth, and to the left and to the right.

14. Kneeling. Put your baby on your lap in the prone position. Hold your baby's thighs in your hands and lift him or her up slowly. Turn your baby around and put their back on your lap in the supine position.

15. Kneeling. Put your baby on your lap. Hold your baby's thighs in your hands and lift him or her up slowly. Turn your baby around and put their back on your lap in the prone position.

1.

2.

3.

16. Sit on the exercise ball while holding your baby. Make circling movements with the ball in both directions.

17. Kneeling. Place your baby on the exercise ball and hold their body. Move the ball forward so that the child puts the soles of their feet on the ground (if your child is not yet standing independently, do not put their feet down). Move backward with the ball until the baby lifts their feet from the ground. Somersault the baby on your shoulder.

1. **2.**

3.

4.

5.

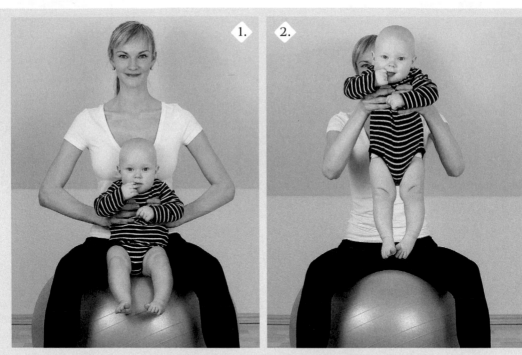

1. **2.**

18. Sit on the exercise ball while holding your baby. Holding their body, lift them forward, to the right and to the left.

3. **4.**

1. 2.

19. Stand up with one hand under your baby's chest and the other between their legs. Play airplane, rock your baby back and forth and move him or her around your body.

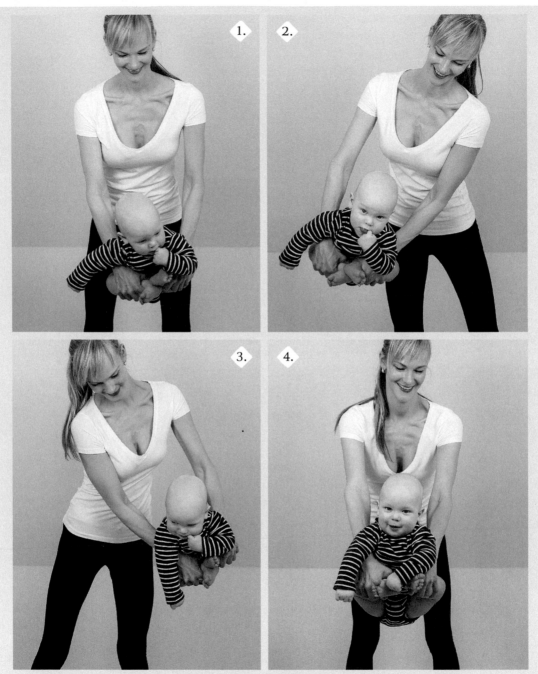

20. Stand up holding your baby's shins. Make sure that the baby's soles are together and your arms are close to their body from trunk to shins. Rock the baby to the right and to the left and back and forth. Make circles or eights.

1.

2.

3.

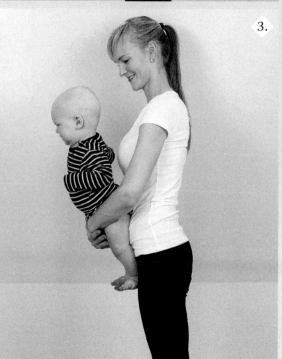

21. Stand up holding your baby with their back to you. Place one hand across the baby's thighs and the other on their chest. Let the baby stoop down and come back up independently by using their back muscles. Take your hand off their chest or make sure that the baby is supporting on your hand very lightly.

1.

1.

2.

22. Stand up and place your baby on your head. Turn to the right and to the left. Slip the baby onto your shoulder, hold their thighs in your hands and put him or her astride your neck. Turn to the right and to the left. Bring the baby's leg on your other shoulder and slip him or her down while supporting their bottom.

3.

4.

5.

23. Stand up holding your baby with their back to you. Holding the baby's body, lean him or her to the right and hold the position for a couple of seconds. Repeat with the other side.

Made in the USA
Las Vegas, NV
23 November 2021

35159632R00093